Healthy Kids

Publications International, Ltd.

Louis Weber, CEO
Publications International, Ltd.
8140 Lehigh Ave
Morton Grove, IL 60053

Pictured on the front cover *(clockwise from top left)*: Meat Loaf Cupcakes *(page 56)*, Sloppy Joe Burritos *(page 70)* and Veggie Pita Pizzas *(page 38)*.

Pictured on the back cover *(clockwise from top left)*: Snake Snacks *(page 86)*, Sunny Mango Sipper *(page 108)*, Mac and Cheese Mini Cups *(page 80)* and Froggy Bento Box *(page 40)*.

ISBN: 978-1-68022-908-0

Manufactured in China.

8 7 6 5 4 3 2 1

Microwave Cooking: Microwave ovens vary in wattage. Use the cooking times as guidelines and check for doneness before adding more time.

Acknowledgments
The publisher would like to thank the organization listed below for the use of their recipe in this publication.
North Dakota Wheat Commission

Table of Contents

Healthy Kids

||||||||||||||||||||||||||||||||||||||||||||||||||||||||||||||||||||||||||||

Dinner doesn't have to be boiled chicken and steamed broccoli to be healthy. Chicken fingers, macaroni and cheese and pancakes can all fit into a healthy eating pattern if you make sure to include plenty of fruits and vegetables and limit unhealthy fats and excess sugar. Even though these things might not seem like health food, they can be when you make them yourself without questionable ingredients and serve them in reasonably sized portions.

Make cooking and eating fun to establish healthy eating habits. To start, let kids pick the recipes. Hand them this book and let them choose what they'd like to eat during the week. Then bring them to the grocery store and let them help you shop for the ingredients. Grocery shopping may seem like drudgery to you, but kids will enjoy picking out produce and taking items from the shelves to put in the cart. If they're old enough, you can even let them help you cook. They'll be more excited to eat their meals if they've helped prepare them, and they'll learn that planning, shopping and cooking can be fun and satisfying.

Adding whimsy to a meal can entice picky eaters to the table. Try "opposite day" and serve chicken fingers or a roll-up sandwich for breakfast and pancakes with a side of fried eggs for dinner. Or try a recipe with a funny ingredient (crushed ramen noodles—that's silly!) to get them to try a new vegetable.

> **NOTE:** This book does not specifically cover food allergies and sensitivities, but many of the recipes can be adapted for special needs. Sometimes it's as easy as using gluten-free pasta or bread instead of regular, or dairy-free milk for regular milk.

Tips for Healthy Eating

||||||||||||||||||||||||||||||||||||||||||||||||||||||||||||||||||||||

• Try to plan three balanced meals a day with several healthy snacks. The recipes in this book are very forgiving so you can make many things ahead of time, or even make double batches to have meals for several days in a row. If you never have time in the morning to make lunches, make them the night before. Sandwiches and wraps will be fine in the fridge for a few days, so you can even get a few days done at once. If breakfast is an issue, make a double batch of pancake batter and make pancakes for several days worth of breakfasts either at night or on a weekend day. Wrap up the leftovers and then heat them up in the oven, toaster or toaster oven as needed. Or make a huge pot of oatmeal and reheat individual portions in the microwave. Smoothies also make fast and easy breakfasts and snacks for the whole family, and are a good option for the days that breakfast needs to happen fast and be consumed on the go.

• Keep carrot sticks, small apples and oranges, bananas and yogurt stocked in your kitchen so that you'll always have a healthy snack ready and won't have to resort to serving junk food. A piece of fruit with a little smear of peanut or other nut butter will make your kids happier than dry packaged cookies or greasy potato chips.

• Try to eat the rainbow every day with a variety of red, orange, yellow, green and blue/purple fruits and vegetables. Depending on the season, rainbow produce may be scarce so head to the frozen aisle. Frozen vegetables make great additions to pasta and grain dishes and frozen fruits are prefect in smoothies or pancakes.

• If necessary, motivate your kids to eat healthy food with the promise of a treat. This book contains a chapter of fruit-filled treats that you can feel good about giving to your kids. You may even find that once they get used to eating healthy, they won't need to promise of something sweet to finish every bite.

Breakfast

Overnight Oatmeal

Makes 6 servings

3 cups water	¼ cup sliced almonds
2 cups chopped peeled apples	½ teaspoon ground cinnamon
1½ cups steel-cut or old-fashioned oats	

Slow Cooker Directions

Combine water, apples, oats, almonds and cinnamon in slow cooker. Cover; cook on LOW 8 hours.

Gluten-Free Buttermilk Pancakes

Makes 4 servings

||||||||||||||||||||||||||||||||||||||||||||||||||||||||||||||||||||||||

- 2 cups gluten-free all-purpose flour blend
- 1½ tablespoons sugar
- 1 teaspoon baking powder
- 1 teaspoon baking soda
- ½ teaspoon salt

- 2¼ cups low-fat buttermilk
- 2 eggs
- 2 tablespoons butter, melted and cooled
- Vegetable oil
- Butter and/or maple syrup

||||||||||||||||||||||||||||||||||||||||||||||||||||||||||||||||||||||||

1. Combine flour blend, sugar, baking powder, baking soda and salt in large bowl. Whisk buttermilk, eggs and 2 tablespoons butter in small bowl. Gradually whisk buttermilk mixture into flour mixture until smooth.

2. Heat griddle or large nonstick skillet over medium heat; brush with oil. Pour batter by ¼ cupfuls 2 inches apart onto griddle. Cook 2 minutes or until lightly browned and edges begin to bubble. Turn over; cook 2 minutes or until lightly browned. Repeat with remaining batter, brushing griddle with additional oil as needed. Serve with additional butter and/or maple syrup.

NOTE: If you do not plan on serving the pancakes right away, keep them warm on a wire rack in a 200°F oven.

Ham & Oinks

Makes 2 servings

||||||||||||||||||||||||||||||||||||||||||||||||||||||||||||||||||||||

2 teaspoons olive oil or butter

2 eggs, beaten

Salt and black pepper

2 crisp corn tostada shells*

¼ cup (1 ounce) shredded Mexican blend cheese (optional)

2 round deli ham slices, plus additional for decoration

Tomato slices

Squeezable yellow mustard

*If prepared tostada shells are not available, crisp regular corn tortillas by brushing with oil and baking in 350°F oven for 10 to 15 minutes.

||||||||||||||||||||||||||||||||||||||||||||||||||||||||||||||||||||||

1. Heat oil in small nonstick skillet over medium-low heat. Add eggs; season with salt and pepper. Scramble 2 to 3 minutes or until firm.

2. Place tostada shells on serving plates. Divide egg mixture between tostada shells. Top eggs with shredded cheese, if desired. Arrange ham slices over eggs. Cut additional ham into triangle shapes for ears. Place oval tomato slice for nose. Use mustard to draw face.

TIP: For breakfast on the go, substitute flour tortillas for the tostada shells and roll up after topping the eggs with the ham.

Strawberry Banana French Toast

Makes 2 to 4 servings

||||||||||||||||||||||||||||||||||||||||||||||||||||||||||||||||||||||

- 1 cup sliced fresh strawberries (about 8 medium)
- 2 teaspoons sugar
- 2 eggs
- ½ cup milk
- 3 tablespoons all-purpose flour
- 1 teaspoon vanilla
- ⅛ teaspoon salt
- 1 tablespoon butter
- 4 slices (1 inch thick) egg bread or country bread
- 1 banana, cut into ¼-inch slices
- Whipped cream, powdered sugar and/or maple syrup (optional)

||||||||||||||||||||||||||||||||||||||||||||||||||||||||||||||||||||||

1. Combine strawberries and sugar in small bowl; toss to coat. Set aside.

2. Whisk eggs, milk, flour, vanilla and salt in shallow bowl or pie plate until well blended. Melt ½ tablespoon butter in large skillet over medium-high heat. Working with two slices at a time, dip bread into egg mixture, turning to coat completely; let excess drip off. Add to skillet; cook 3 to 4 minutes per side or until golden brown. Repeat with remaining butter and bread slices.

3. Top each serving with strawberry mixture and banana slices. Garnish with whipped cream, powdered sugar or maple syrup.

Banana Chocolate Chip Buttermilk Pancakes

Makes 6 to 8 servings

||||||||||||||||||||||||||||||||||||||||||||||||||||||||||||||||||||||||||

2½ cups gluten-free all-purpose flour blend or all-purpose flour

⅓ cup sugar

1½ teaspoons baking powder

1 teaspoon baking soda

½ teaspoon ground cinnamon

1½ cups buttermilk

3 eggs

1 teaspoon vanilla

1½ cups mashed bananas (about 3 medium)

Vegetable oil

¾ cup milk chocolate chips, plus additional for garnish

Butter and/or maple syrup

||||||||||||||||||||||||||||||||||||||||||||||||||||||||||||||||||||||||||

1. Combine flour blend, sugar, baking powder, baking soda and cinnamon in large bowl. Whisk buttermilk, eggs and vanilla in medium bowl. Gradually whisk buttermilk mixture into flour mixture until smooth. Fold in bananas.

2. Heat griddle or large skillet over medium heat; brush with oil. Pour batter by ¼ cupfuls 2 inches apart onto griddle. Place about 10 chocolate chips on each pancake. Cook 2 to 3 minutes or until lightly browned and edges begin to bubble. Turn over; cook 2 minutes or until lightly browned. Repeat with remaining batter and chocolate chips, brushing griddle with additional oil as needed. Serve with butter and/or maple syrup. Top with additional chocolate chips.

Banana Split Breakfast Bowl

Makes 4 servings

||||||||||||||||||||||||||||||||||||||||||||||||||||||||||||||||||||||

2½ tablespoons sliced almonds

2½ tablespoons chopped walnuts

3 cups vanilla nonfat yogurt

1⅓ cups sliced fresh strawberries

2 bananas, halved or sliced

½ cup drained pineapple tidbits

||||||||||||||||||||||||||||||||||||||||||||||||||||||||||||||||||||||

1. Spread almonds and walnuts in single layer in small heavy skillet. Cook and stir over medium heat 2 minutes or until lightly browned. Immediately remove from skillet; cool completely.

2. Spoon yogurt into serving bowl. Layer with strawberries, bananas and pineapple. Sprinkle with toasted almonds and walnuts.

NOTE: Breakfast is a great time to eat one of the two recommended fruit servings for the day. There's no need to put aside your favorite recipes until berry season comes around; recipes like this one can be made with fresh or frozen strawberries. Frozen fruits are economical, convenient and available year-round—they are harvested at their peak of ripeness and can be stored in the freezer for 8 to 12 months.

Breakfast Pizza Margherita

Makes 6 servings

||||||||||||||||||||||||||||||||||||||||||||||||||||||||||||

1 (12-inch) prepared pizza crust

3 slices turkey bacon

8 eggs, beaten

½ cup milk

1½ tablespoons chopped fresh basil, divided

⅛ teaspoon black pepper

2 plum tomatoes, thinly sliced

½ cup (2 ounces) shredded mozzarella cheese

¼ cup (1 ounce) shredded Cheddar cheese

||||||||||||||||||||||||||||||||||||||||||||||||||||||||||||

1. Preheat oven to 450°F. Place pizza crust on 12-inch pizza pan. Bake 6 to 8 minutes or until heated through.

2. Meanwhile, spray large skillet with nonstick cooking spray. Add bacon; cook over medium-high heat until crisp. Drain on paper towels. Crumble bacon when cool enough to handle.

3. Combine eggs, milk, ½ tablespoon basil and pepper in medium bowl. Coat same skillet with cooking spray. Add egg mixture; cook over medium heat until mixture begins to set around edges. Gently stir eggs, allowing uncooked portions to flow underneath. Repeat stirring 1 to 2 minutes or until eggs are just set. Remove from heat.

4. Arrange tomato slices on pizza crust. Spoon scrambled eggs over tomatoes. Sprinkle with bacon and cheeses. Bake 1 minute or until cheeses are melted. Sprinkle with remaining 1 tablespoon basil. Cut into wedges. Serve immediately.

Whole Wheat Pancakes

Makes 4 servings

||||||||||||||||||||||||||||||||||||||||||||||||||||||||||||||||||

¾ cup milk

2 eggs

¼ cup plain nonfat Greek yogurt

2 tablespoons vegetable oil

1 tablespoon honey

1 cup whole wheat flour

2 teaspoons baking powder

⅛ teaspoon salt

2 teaspoons butter

Fresh raspberries, blueberries and/or strawberries

Maple syrup or agave nectar (optional)

||||||||||||||||||||||||||||||||||||||||||||||||||||||||||||||||||

1. Whisk milk, eggs, yogurt, oil and honey in medium bowl until well blended. Add flour, baking powder and salt; whisk just until blended.

2. Heat large nonstick skillet over medium heat. Add 1 teaspoon butter; brush to evenly coat skillet. Drop batter by ¼ cupfuls into skillet. Cook about 2 minutes or until tops of pancakes appear dull and bubbles form around edges. Turn over; cook 1 to 2 minutes or until firm and lightly browned. Repeat with remaining batter, adding remaining 1 teaspoon butter as needed.

3. Serve with berries and maple syrup, if desired.

Scrambled Egg and Red Pepper Pockets

Makes 2 servings

||||||||||||||||||||||||||||||||||||||||||||||||||||||||||||||||

1 egg

2 egg whites

1 tablespoon milk

⅛ teaspoon salt

⅛ teaspoon black pepper

1½ teaspoons butter, softened and divided

3 tablespoons minced red onion

2 tablespoons diced jarred roasted red pepper (blot before dicing)

1 whole wheat pita bread round, cut in half crosswise

||||||||||||||||||||||||||||||||||||||||||||||||||||||||||||||||

1. Whisk egg, egg whites, milk, salt and black pepper in small bowl until well blended.

2. Spray medium skillet with nonstick cooking spray. Add ½ teaspoon butter; heat over medium heat. Add onion; cook and stir 3 to 5 minutes or until lightly browned. Pour egg mixture into skillet; sprinkle with red peppers. Stir gently, lifting edge to allow uncooked portion to flow underneath. Continue cooking until set.

3. Evenly spread inside of each pita half with remaining 1 teaspoon butter. Spoon egg mixture into pita halves.

> **NOTE:** An ideal breakfast includes lean protein, complex carbohydrates and a little bit of fat. This recipe includes all these important elements, and it's filling enough to get you through the morning. Plus, it's fast and easy to make!

Oatmeal Waffles with Spiced Apple Compote

Makes 6 servings

||||||||||||||||||||||||||||||||||||||||||||||||||||||||||||||||||||||||||

Apple Compote

- 2 tablespoons butter
- 1 pound Granny Smith apples, peeled, cored and cut into ½-inch pieces
- ¼ cup maple syrup
- ½ cup water
- ¼ cup raisins
- 1 teaspoon ground cinnamon

Waffles

- 1¼ cups quick-cooking oats
- ¾ cup oat flour
- ¼ cup flax meal
- 1 tablespoon baking powder
- ½ teaspoon salt
- 1¾ cups hot milk
- ½ cup (1 stick) butter, melted and slightly cooled
- 3 eggs
- ¼ cup maple syrup

||||||||||||||||||||||||||||||||||||||||||||||||||||||||||||||||||||||||||

1. Preheat Belgium waffle maker to medium-high heat. Set wire rack on top of large baking sheet. Preheat oven to 200°F.

2. For apple compote, melt 2 tablespoons butter in large nonstick skillet over medium-high heat. Add apples, ¼ cup maple syrup, water, raisins and cinnamon; stir to combine. Reduce heat to medium; cover and cook 5 minutes. Uncover and cook 5 minutes or until apples are tender and most liquid has evaporated, stirring occasionally. Set aside.

3. For waffles, combine oats, flour, flax meal, baking powder and salt in large bowl. Pour in hot milk; stir until combined. Let stand 5 minutes.

4. Whisk melted butter, eggs and ¼ cup maple syrup in medium bowl. Pour into oat mixture; stir until combined.

5. Pour ⅓ cup batter into each well of waffle maker. Close lid; cook 6 minutes or until golden brown. Remove waffles to wire rack in oven; tent with foil to keep warm. Repeat with remaining batter. Serve waffles with apple compote.

Denver Scramble in Hash Brown Cups

Makes 12 cups (4 to 6 servings)

||||||||||||||||||||||||||||||||||||||||||||||||||||||||||||||||||||

3 tablespoons butter, divided

1 package (20 ounces) refrigerated hash brown potatoes

1½ teaspoons salt, divided

6 eggs

2 tablespoons milk

⅛ teaspoon black pepper

⅛ teaspoon hot pepper sauce

½ cup diced onion (¼-inch pieces)

½ cup diced green bell pepper (¼-inch pieces)

½ cup diced ham (¼-inch pieces)

⅓ cup shredded Monterey Jack cheese

||||||||||||||||||||||||||||||||||||||||||||||||||||||||||||||||||||

1. Preheat oven to 400°F. Spray 12 standard (2½-inch) muffin cups with nonstick cooking spray.

2. Melt 2 tablespoons butter. Combine melted butter, potatoes and 1 teaspoon salt in large bowl; toss to coat. Press potatoes into bottoms and up sides of prepared cups (about 5 to 6 tablespoons per cup).

3. Bake about 35 minutes or until bottoms and sides are golden brown. (Insides of cups will not brown.)

4. When hash brown cups have baked 15 minutes, beat eggs, milk, remaining ½ teaspoon salt, black pepper and hot pepper sauce in medium bowl until well blended. Melt remaining 1 tablespoon butter in large skillet over medium-high heat. Add onion; cook and stir about 4 minutes or until softened.

Add bell pepper; cook and stir 4 minutes. Add ham; cook and stir 5 minutes or until bell pepper is crisp-tender. Pour egg mixture into skillet; cook 20 to 30 seconds without stirring or just until edges are beginning to set. Stir around edges and across bottom of skillet with heatproof spatula, forming large curds. Cook 3 to 4 minutes or until eggs are fluffy and barely set, stirring gently.

5. Remove hash brown cups from pan. Fill cups with scrambled egg mixture (about ¼ cup egg mixture per cup); sprinkle with cheese.

Lunch

Turkey and Veggie Roll-Ups

Makes 2 servings

2 tablespoons hummus, any flavor

1 (8-inch) whole wheat tortilla

¼ cup sliced baby spinach

2 slices oven-roasted turkey breast (about 1 ounce)

¼ cup thinly sliced English cucumber

1 slice (1 ounce) Swiss cheese

¼ cup thinly sliced carrot

Spread hummus on tortilla to within 1 inch of edge. Layer with spinach, turkey, cucumber, cheese and carrot. Roll up tortilla and filling; cut into four pieces.

Bavarian Pretzel Sandwiches

Makes 4 sandwiches

4 frozen soft pretzels, thawed	8 slices Black Forest ham
1 tablespoon German mustard	4 slices Gouda cheese
2 teaspoons mayonnaise	1 tablespoon water
	Coarse pretzel salt

1. Preheat oven to 350°F. Line baking sheet with parchment paper.

2. Carefully slice each pretzel in half crosswise using serrated knife. Combine mustard and mayonnaise in small bowl. Spread mustard mixture onto bottom halves of pretzels. Top with 2 slices ham, 1 slice cheese and top halves of pretzels.

3. Place sandwiches on prepared baking sheet. Brush tops of sandwiches with water; sprinkle with salt. Bake 8 minutes or until cheese is melted.

TIP: To make these sandwiches for packed lunch, bake pretzels according to package directions. Cut baked pretzels in half and make sandwiches.

Ham Roll Bento Box

Makes 1 bento box

||||||||||||||||||||||||||||||||||||||||||||||||||||||||||||||||||||

⅔ cup uncooked sushi rice

1 cup water

2 teaspoons sugar

⅛ teaspoon salt

2 tablespoons rice vinegar

2 slices deli ham (about 4 inches long)

1 roasted bell pepper, cut into strips

Honey mustard

1 small cucumber, sliced

Hummus and halved grape tomatoes

Carrot sticks and/or fresh fruit

||||||||||||||||||||||||||||||||||||||||||||||||||||||||||||||||||||

1. Place rice in fine mesh strainer; rinse under cold water. Place in small saucepan; stir in 1 cup water. Bring to a simmer; cover and cook 12 minutes or until water is absorbed and rice is tender. Remove from heat. Cover and let stand 10 minutes.

2. Combine sugar, salt and vinegar in small saucepan. Bring to a simmer; cook and stir until sugar is dissolved. Pour over rice and mix gently. Set aside to cool.

3. Place 1 ham slice on work surface. Spread about 2 tablespoons rice evenly down center of each ham slice. Arrange pepper strip over rice. Tightly roll into 4-inch tube. Repeat with remaining ham slice, rice and bell pepper. Cut each ham roll into bite-size pieces. Pack one section of bento box with ham rolls and container of honey mustard for dipping.

4. Make cucumber flowers by spreading hummus on cucumber slices. Top with halved tomatoes. Pack rice into another compartment; top with cucumber flowers. Include vegetables and fruit in other compartments.

Tasty Turkey Turnovers

Makes 8 servings

||||||||||||||||||||||||||||||||||||||||||||||||||||||||||||||||

8 frozen dinner rolls, thawed according to package directions

2 tablespoons honey mustard

3 ounces thinly sliced deli turkey

¾ cup packaged broccoli coleslaw

1 egg white, beaten

||||||||||||||||||||||||||||||||||||||||||||||||||||||||||||||||

1. Preheat oven to 425°F. Spray baking sheet with nonstick cooking spray.

2. Place rolls on lightly floured surface. Roll each dinner roll into 3½-inch circle with lightly floured rolling pin. Spread honey mustard lightly over dough; top with turkey and coleslaw. Brush edges of dough with beaten egg white. Fold dough in half; press edges with tines of fork to seal.

3. Place turnovers on prepared baking sheet; brush with egg white. Bake about 15 minutes or until golden brown. Let stand 5 minutes before serving. Serve warm or at room temperature.

Chicken Tzatziki Pitas

Makes 4 servings

||||||||||||||||||||||||||||||||||||||||||||||||||||||||||||||||||

½ cup plain nonfat Greek yogurt

¼ cup finely chopped cucumber

2 teaspoons lemon juice

2 teaspoons chopped fresh mint

1 clove garlic, crushed

¼ teaspoon salt

Dash black pepper

1 cup chopped cooked chicken

1 cup chopped romaine lettuce

½ cup chopped tomatoes

2 tablespoons chopped red onion

2 tablespoons chopped Greek olives

4 (6-inch) whole wheat pita halves

||||||||||||||||||||||||||||||||||||||||||||||||||||||||||||||||||

1. Stir together yogurt, cucumber, lemon juice, mint, garlic, salt and pepper in small bowl; set aside.

2. Divide chicken, lettuce, tomatoes, onion and olives evenly among pita halves. Drizzle with sauce.

PACKING TIP: Stir the chicken, tomatoes, onion and olives into the tzatziki sauce before stuffing it into the pita halves. Line the pita halves with lettuce and fill with chicken mixture. Place each filled pita half in a resealable sandwich bag. Press out as much air as possible before sealing the bag.

Veggie Pizza Pitas

Makes 4 servings

||||||||||||||||||||||||||||||||||||||||||||||||||||||||||||||

- 2 whole wheat pita bread rounds, cut in half horizontally (to make 4 rounds)
- ¼ cup pizza sauce
- 1 teaspoon dried basil
- ⅛ teaspoon red pepper flakes (optional)
- 1 cup sliced mushrooms
- ½ cup thinly sliced green bell pepper
- ½ cup thinly sliced red onion
- 1 cup (4 ounces) shredded mozzarella cheese
- 2 teaspoons grated Parmesan cheese

||||||||||||||||||||||||||||||||||||||||||||||||||||||||||||||

1. Preheat oven to 475°F.

2. Arrange pita rounds, rough sides up, in single layer on large nonstick baking sheet. Spread 1 tablespoon pizza sauce evenly over each pita round to within ¼ inch of edge. Sprinkle with basil and red pepper flakes, if desired. Top with mushrooms, bell pepper and onion. Sprinkle with mozzarella cheese.

3. Bake 5 minutes or until mozzarella cheese is melted. Sprinkle ½ teaspoon Parmesan cheese over each pita round.

Froggy Bento Box

Makes 1 bento box

||||||||||||||||||||||||||||||||||||||||||||||||||||||||||||||||||

½ cup uncooked sushi rice or other short grain rice

¾ cup water

¼ teaspoon salt

1 drop blue paste food coloring

Assorted sliced lunch meat

1 seedless cucumber

Prepared ranch dressing or Dairy-Free Ranch Dressing (page 41)

Carrot slices, cut into fish shapes

Assorted raw vegetables, such as lettuce, celery sticks, pea pods and grape tomatoes

||||||||||||||||||||||||||||||||||||||||||||||||||||||||||||||||||

1. Place rice in fine mesh strainer; rinse under cold water for 1 minute. Combine rice, ¾ cup water, salt and food coloring in small heavy saucepan; bring to a simmer. Reduce heat to low; cover and cook 15 minutes or until water is absorbed and rice is tender. Remove from heat. Cover and let stand 10 minutes.

2. For lily pond, fill bottom of one section of bento box with blue rice. (Refrigerate extra rice for another use.) To make lily pads, cut small circles from lunch meat. Cut cucumber into small rounds. Make stacks of meat and cucumber rounds with small dabs of ranch dressing between layers. Position lily pads on blue rice. Place carrot fish between lily pads.

3. Line second section of bento box with lettuce and arrange raw vegetables and additional dressing in small container. (Refrigerate remaining dressing for another use.)

DAIRY-FREE RANCH DRESSING:

Whisk 4 teaspoons soymilk and ¾ teaspoon lemon juice in small bowl; let stand 10 minutes. Whisk 1 cup vegan mayonnaise, 1 tablespoon chopped fresh parsley, 1 tablespoon chopped fresh chives, ½ teaspoon dried dill weed, ¼ teaspoon onion powder, ¼ teaspoon salt and ⅛ teaspoon black pepper in medium bowl. Whisk in soymilk mixture. Cover and refrigerate 30 minutes.

Grilled Buffalo Chicken Wraps

Makes 4 servings

||||||||||||||||||||||||||||||||||||||||||||||||||||||||||||||||||||

- 1 pound boneless skinless chicken breasts
- ¼ cup plus 2 tablespoons buffalo wing sauce, divided
- 2 cups broccoli slaw
- 1 tablespoon blue cheese salad dressing
- 4 (8-inch) whole wheat tortillas, warmed

||||||||||||||||||||||||||||||||||||||||||||||||||||||||||||||||||||

1. Place chicken in large resealable food storage bag. Add ¼ cup buffalo sauce; seal bag. Marinate in refrigerator 15 minutes.

2. Meanwhile, prepare grill for direct cooking over medium-high heat. Grill chicken 5 to 6 minutes per side or until no longer pink. When cool enough to handle, slice chicken and toss with remaining 2 tablespoons buffalo sauce in medium bowl.

3. Combine broccoli slaw and blue cheese dressing in medium bowl; mix well.

4. Arrange chicken and broccoli slaw evenly down center of each tortilla. Roll up to secure filling. To serve, cut in half diagonally.

TIP: If you don't like the spicy flavor of buffalo wing sauce, substitute your favorite barbecue sauce.

Wild Wedges

Makes 4 servings

|||||||||||||||||||||||||||||||||||||||||||||||||||||||||||||||

2 (8-inch) flour tortillas

⅓ cup shredded Cheddar cheese

⅓ cup chopped cooked chicken or turkey

1 green onion, thinly sliced

2 tablespoons mild thick and chunky salsa

|||||||||||||||||||||||||||||||||||||||||||||||||||||||||||||||

1. Heat large nonstick skillet over medium heat; spray with nonstick cooking spray.

2. Place one tortilla in skillet. Top with cheese, chicken, green onion and salsa and second tortilla.

3. Cook 2 to 3 minutes per side or until golden brown and cheese is melted. Remove from skillet and cut into eight wedges.

VARIATION: For bean quesadillas, omit the chicken and spread ⅓ cup canned refried beans over one of the tortillas.

Chicken and Grape Pita Sandwiches

Makes 6 servings

||||||||||||||||||||||||||||||||||||||||||||||||||||||||||||||||||||

- 1 quart water
- 1 pound boneless skinless chicken breasts, cut into ½-inch pieces
- ½ cup plain nonfat yogurt
- ¼ cup mayonnaise
- 2 tablespoons fresh tarragon, minced *or* 2 teaspoons dried tarragon
- 2 teaspoons Dijon mustard
- 2 teaspoons honey
- ½ teaspoon black pepper
- 1 cup thinly sliced celery
- 1 cup red seedless grapes, cut into halves
- 1 medium head red leaf lettuce
- 3 pita bread rounds, cut in half crosswise

||||||||||||||||||||||||||||||||||||||||||||||||||||||||||||||||||||

1. Bring water to a boil in large saucepan. Add chicken; cover and remove from heat. Let stand 6 minutes or until chicken is cooked through (165°F). Drain and rinse chicken under cold water.

2. Stir yogurt, mayonnaise, tarragon, mustard, honey and pepper in large bowl until well blended. Add chicken, celery and grapes; toss to coat evenly. Separate lettuce leaves. Select six large leaves and discard stems. Tear or shred remaining leaves.

3. Line each pita half with whole lettuce leaf. Fill with handful of torn lettuce leaves and about ⅔ cup chicken mixture.

Meal in a Bun

Makes 18 buns

|||||||||||||||||||||||||||||||||||||||||||||||||||||||||||||||||||||||||

| 2 | pounds frozen bread dough | 1 | recipe Tostado Filling or Pizza Filling (recipes follow) |

|||||||||||||||||||||||||||||||||||||||||||||||||||||||||||||||||||||||||

Thaw dough until warm. On lightly floured board, roll each 1-pound loaf into 12-inch square. Cut each into nine 4-inch square pieces. In center of each square, spoon 2 tablespoons filling. Pick up corners of each square and pinch together. Pinch each diagonal seam so edges are well sealed. Place on baking sheet coated with nonstick cooking spray. Bake at 400°F for 15 to 18 minutes. Serve warm.

NOTES:
Leftovers may be frozen; wrap in foil and reheat at 350°F for 20 minutes or until hot in center.

Buns may be frozen and placed in airtight container. To serve, place on baking sheet coated with nonstick cooking spray and bake at 350°F until browned, about 35 minutes.

Pizza Filling

| 1 | pound extra-lean ground beef | ½ | cup pizza sauce |
| ¼ | cup minced onion | 1 | cup mozzarella cheese |

Cook ground beef and onion over medium heat, until beef is no longer pink: drain thoroughly. Stir in pizza sauce and cheese.

Tostado Filling

1 pound extra-lean
   ground beef
¼ cup minced onion
1 cup shredded Cheddar
   cheese

½ cup tomato sauce
1 package taco
   seasoning mix

Cook ground beef and onion over medium heat until beef is
no longer pink; drain thoroughly. Stir in cheese, tomato sauce
and taco seasoning.

Favorite recipes from North Dakota Wheat Commission

Birch Bark Sandwich

Makes 1 serving

|||||||||||||||||||||||||||||||||||||||||||||||||||||||||||||||||||

- 1 (10-inch) flour tortilla
- 1 tablespoon
    mayonnaise
- 1 teaspoon mustard
- 4 slices deli ham

|||||||||||||||||||||||||||||||||||||||||||||||||||||||||||||||||||

1. Spread one side of tortilla with mayonnaise and mustard. Lay ham slices on tortilla, overlapping to cover, leaving about 2 inches uncovered at top of tortilla. Tightly roll tortilla, forming a log.

2. Cut in half to serve.

Dinner

Waffled Burger Sliders

Makes 8 sliders

8 ounces ground beef

½ teaspoon salt

Black pepper

8 slider buns *or* 4 slices bread, cut into quarters and toasted

1 tablespoon butter, melted

Toppings: lettuce, tomatoes, cheese, pickles and/or ketchup

1. Combine beef and salt in large bowl. Season with pepper. Shape into eight small patties.

2. Heat waffle maker to medium. Brush buns with melted butter; set aside.

3. Place 4 patties at a time in waffle maker. Cook about 3 minutes or until cooked through. Serve patties on buns with desired toppings.

Veggie-Packed Spaghetti and Meatballs

Makes 4 servings

||||||||||||||||||||||||||||||||||||||||||||||||||||||||||||||||||||||||||||

- 4 ounces uncooked spaghetti or vermicelli
- 12 ounces ground turkey or beef
- 1 package (10 ounces) frozen chopped spinach, thawed and pressed dry
- ½ cup fresh whole wheat bread crumbs*
- 1 egg white

- 1 teaspoon onion powder
- 1 teaspoon garlic powder
- ½ teaspoon *each* salt and black pepper
- 2 cups pasta sauce
- 2 cups small broccoli florets
- ½ cup packaged julienned carrots

*To make fresh bread crumbs, tear 1 slice bread into pieces; process in food processor until coarse crumbs form.

||||||||||||||||||||||||||||||||||||||||||||||||||||||||||||||||||||||||||||

1. Cook spaghetti according to package directions; return to saucepan and keep warm.

2. Meanwhile, combine turkey, spinach, bread crumbs, egg white, onion powder, garlic powder, salt and pepper in medium bowl; mix well. Shape into 32 (½-inch) meatballs.

3. Spray large skillet with nonstick cooking spray; heat over medium heat. Add meatballs; cook 8 to 10 minutes, turning to brown all sides.

4. Add pasta sauce, broccoli and carrots to skillet. Cover; bring to a simmer over medium-low heat. Cook 8 to 10 minutes or until vegetables are tender and sauce is heated through. Serve sauce and meatballs over spaghetti.

Meat Loaf Cupcakes

Makes 10 servings

‖‖‖

- 3 medium potatoes, peeled and chopped
- 1½ pounds 90% lean ground beef
- ½ cup finely chopped onion
- ⅓ cup old-fashioned oats
- 1 egg
- 2 tablespoons chopped fresh rosemary
- 1¼ teaspoons salt, divided
- ½ teaspoon black pepper, divided
- ½ cup milk
- 2 tablespoons butter
- ¼ cup snipped fresh chives

‖‖‖

1. Preheat oven to 350°F. Place potatoes in medium saucepan; cover with water. Bring to a boil; cook 25 to 30 minutes or until potatoes are fork-tender.

2. Combine beef, onion, oats, egg, rosemary, ¼ teaspoon salt and ¼ teaspoon pepper in large bowl; mix well. Divide mixture among 10 standard (2½-inch) muffin cups or silicone liners.

3. Bake 25 minutes or until cooked through (160°F). Meanwhile, beat potatoes, milk, butter, remaining 1 teaspoon salt and ¼ teaspoon pepper in large bowl with electric mixer at medium speed 3 minutes or until smooth. Place mashed potato mixture in large piping bag fitted with large star tip.

4. Pipe mashed potatoes over meat loaves. Sprinkle with chives.

Pork Tenderloin Sliders

Makes 12 sandwiches

2 teaspoons chili powder

¾ teaspoon ground cumin

½ teaspoon salt

½ teaspoon black pepper

2 tablespoons olive oil, divided

2 pork tenderloins (about 1 pound each)

12 green onions, ends trimmed

½ cup mayonnaise

1 canned chipotle pepper in adobo sauce, minced*

2 teaspoons lime juice

12 dinner rolls, sliced in half horizontally

12 slices Monterey Jack cheese

If chipotles are too spicy for your kids, just use plain mayonnaise or mix mayonnaise with 1 tablespoon yellow mustard.

1. Prepare grill for direct cooking over medium heat.

2. Combine chili powder, cumin, salt and black pepper in small bowl. Rub 1 tablespoon oil evenly over pork. Sprinkle cumin mixture evenly over tenderloins; turn to coat. Coat green onions with remaining 1 tablespoon oil.

3. Combine mayonnaise, chipotle pepper and lime juice is small bowl. Cover and refrigerate.

4. Grill pork, covered, 15 minutes or until 160°F, turning occasionally. Remove to cutting board. Tent with foil; let stand 10 minutes.

5. Meanwhile, grill green onions 3 minutes or until browned, turning frequently.

6. Coarsely chop green onions. Thinly slice pork. Evenly spread chipotle mayonnaise on bottom halves of rolls. Top with green onions, tenderloin slices and cheese. Replace roll tops. Serve immediately.

Macaroni and Cheese with Mixed Vegetables

Makes 4 servings

||||||||||||||||||||||||||||||||||||||||||||||||||||||||||||||||||

1¼ cups milk, divided

2 tablespoons all-purpose flour

½ cup (2 ounces) shredded Cheddar cheese, divided

½ cup shredded Parmesan cheese, divided

1½ cups frozen mixed vegetables, cooked and drained

1⅓ cups cooked whole wheat elbow macaroni, rotini or penne

¼ teaspoon salt

⅛ teaspoon black pepper

||||||||||||||||||||||||||||||||||||||||||||||||||||||||||||||||||

1. Preheat oven to 325°F. Coat 1½-quart baking dish with nonstick cooking spray.

2. Stir ¼ cup milk and flour in medium saucepan until smooth. Add remaining 1 cup milk; stir until well blended. Cook, stirring constantly over medium heat until thickened.

3. Stir ¼ cup Cheddar cheese and ¼ cup Parmesan cheese into saucepan. Add vegetables, macaroni, salt and pepper.

4. Spoon macaroni mixture into prepared baking dish. Sprinkle with remaining ¼ cup Cheddar cheese and ¼ cup Parmesan cheese. Bake 20 minutes or until cheeses are melted and macaroni is heated through. Let stand 5 minutes before serving.

Fish and "Chips"

Makes 4 servings

||||||||||||||||||||||||||||||||||||||||||||||||||||||||||||||||||||||||

3 cups gluten-free crisp rice cereal, divided

1 egg

1 tablespoon water

1 pound cod, haddock or other firm white fish fillets, cut into 2×4-inch strips

1½ teaspoons dried Italian seasoning, divided

Salt and black pepper

2 tablespoons butter, melted

2 medium zucchini, cut into sticks

1 package (8 ounces) carrot sticks

1 tablespoon olive oil

||||||||||||||||||||||||||||||||||||||||||||||||||||||||||||||||||||||||

1. Preheat oven to 350°F. Spray large baking sheet with nonstick cooking spray or line with foil.

2. Place 2 cups cereal in resealable food storage bag; coarsely crush with rolling pin. Combine with remaining 1 cup cereal in large shallow dish. Beat egg and water in separate shallow dish.

3. Sprinkle fish with 1 teaspoon Italian seasoning and season with salt and pepper. Dip in egg, letting excess drip back into dish. Coat in cereal, pressing lightly to adhere. Place on prepared baking sheet. Drizzle with butter.

4. Place zucchini and carrot sticks on same baking sheet in single layer. Drizzle with oil and sprinkle with remaining ½ teaspoon Italian seasoning. Season with salt and pepper.

5. Bake 20 to 25 minutes or until fish is opaque in center and vegetables are tender.

Polka Dot Lasagna Skillet

Makes 4 to 6 servings

||||||||||||||||||||||||||||||||||||||||||||||||||||||||||||||||||||||||||||||

1 pound ground turkey or beef

8 ounces uncooked mafalda or cellantani pasta

2 cups marinara pasta sauce

4 cups hot water

½ cup ricotta cheese

1 egg

3 tablespoons grated Parmesan cheese

2 tablespoons all-purpose flour

2 tablespoons chopped fresh Italian parsley

½ teaspoon dried Italian seasoning

¼ teaspoon black pepper

||||||||||||||||||||||||||||||||||||||||||||||||||||||||||||||||||||||||||||||

1. Cook turkey in large skillet over medium-high heat or until no longer pink, stirring to break up meat.

2. Stir in pasta, marinara and hot water; bring to a boil. Reduce heat to low; cover and cook 10 minutes.

3. Meanwhile, blend ricotta, egg, Parmesan, flour, parsley, Italian seasoning and pepper in small bowl until smooth. Drop tablespoonfuls of ricotta mixture over pasta; cover and cook 4 to 5 minutes or until dumplings are set. Remove from heat; let stand 5 minutes before serving.

Mexicali Tortilla Skillet

Makes 4 servings

||||||||||||||||||||||||||||||||||||||||||||||||||||||||||||||||||

12 ounces extra lean ground beef

2 poblano peppers, seeded and chopped

1 cup diced onion

12 ounces ripe tomatoes, chopped (about 3 medium)

1 tablespoon ground cumin

2 teaspoons paprika

2 to 3 teaspoons sugar

½ teaspoon salt

2 ounces corn tortilla chips, coarsely crumbled

¼ cup (1 ounce) shredded sharp Cheddar cheese

½ ripe avocado, chopped

¼ cup chopped fresh cilantro

¼ cup sour cream

1 lime, quartered

||||||||||||||||||||||||||||||||||||||||||||||||||||||||||||||||||

1. Cook and stir beef in large nonstick skillet over medium-high heat 2 minutes. Stir in peppers and onion; cook and stir 4 minutes or until vegetables are soft. Stir in tomatoes, cumin, paprika and sugar; bring to a boil. Reduce heat; cover and simmer 5 to 10 minutes or until tomatoes are tender. Remove from heat; stir in salt.

2. Top with tortilla chips, cheese, avocado and cilantro. Serve with sour cream and lime wedges.

Chicken Nuggets with Tomato Dipping Sauce

Makes 4 servings

Tomato Dipping Sauce (page 69)

1 package (3 ounces) ramen noodles, any flavor,* finely crushed**

½ cup panko bread crumbs

½ cup grated Parmesan cheese

1 teaspoon garlic powder

1 teaspoon dried basil

½ teaspoon salt

¼ teaspoon black pepper

1 egg, lightly beaten

1½ pounds boneless skinless chicken breasts, cut into 1×2½-inch pieces

½ cup vegetable oil

*Discard seasoning packet.

**Or substitute an additional 1 cup panko bread crumbs.

1. Prepare Tomato Dipping Sauce; set aside. Combine ramen, panko, cheese, garlic powder, basil, salt and pepper in large bowl. Place egg in shallow dish. Dip chicken in egg; shake off excess. Coat with panko mixture.

2. Heat oil in large skillet over medium heat. Cook chicken in batches about 5 minutes or until cooked through, turning once. Serve with Tomato Dipping Sauce.

Tomato Dipping Sauce
Makes 1½ cups

1 tablespoon olive oil	1 can (about 14 ounces) fire-roasted diced tomatoes
1 small onion, chopped	
2 cloves garlic, minced	
⅛ to ¼ teaspoon ground red pepper	

1. Heat oil in medium skillet. Add onion and garlic; cook and stir about 3 minutes or until onion is tender and golden brown. Stir in ground red pepper.

2. Remove skillet from heat; add tomatoes. Process in blender or food processor until smooth. Return to skillet and cook about 10 minutes or until thickened and reduced to 1½ cups.

Sloppy Joe Burritos

Makes 4 servings

||||||||||||||||||||||||||||||||||||||||||||||||||||||||||||||||

- 1 tablespoon cider vinegar
- 1 teaspoon sugar
- 1 teaspoon vegetable oil
- ¼ teaspoon salt
- 2 cups coleslaw mix
- 1 pound ground beef
- 1 can (about 16 ounces) sloppy joe sauce
- 1 cup *each* chopped red and green bell peppers
- ½ cup chopped onion
- 4 (7- to 8-inch) spinach or regular tortillas

||||||||||||||||||||||||||||||||||||||||||||||||||||||||||||||||

1. Whisk vinegar, sugar, oil and salt in medium bowl until well blended. Add coleslaw mix; toss to coat. Set aside.

2. Brown beef in large skillet over medium-high heat 6 to 8 minutes, stirring to break up meat. Drain fat. Stir in sloppy joe sauce; cook over low heat about 3 minutes or until slightly thickened.

3. Add bell peppers and onion; cook and stir 2 to 3 minutes. Reduce heat to low; cook 3 minutes or until vegetables are tender.

4. Divide meat mixture evenly among tortillas. Top each with ½ cup coleslaw mixture. Roll up tortillas, folding in sides to enclose filling.

Tuna-Macaroni Casserole

Makes 6 servings

||||||||||||||||||||||||||||||||||||||||||||||||||||||||||||||||||||||||||||||||||

1 cup mayonnaise

1 cup (4 ounces) shredded Swiss cheese

½ cup milk

¼ cup chopped onion

¼ cup chopped red bell pepper

⅛ teaspoon black pepper

2 cans (about 6 ounces each) tuna, drained and flaked

1 package (about 10 ounces) frozen peas

2 cups shell pasta or elbow macaroni, cooked and drained

½ cup panko or plain dry bread crumbs

2 tablespoons melted butter

Chopped fresh parsley (optional)

||||||||||||||||||||||||||||||||||||||||||||||||||||||||||||||||||||||||||||||||||

1. Preheat oven to 350°F.

2. Combine mayonnaise, cheese, milk, onion, bell pepper and black pepper in large bowl. Add tuna, peas and pasta; toss to coat well. Spoon into 2-quart casserole.

3. Mix panko with butter in small bowl; sprinkle over top of casserole. Bake 30 to 40 minutes or until panko is golden brown and casserole is heated through. Top with chopped parsley, if desired.

Sandwich Monsters

Makes 7 sandwiches

||||||||||||||||||||||||||||||||||||||||||||||||||||||||||||||||||||||

1 package (about 16 ounces) refrigerated jumbo buttermilk biscuits (8 biscuits)

1 cup (4 ounces) shredded mozzarella cheese

⅓ cup sliced mushrooms

2 ounces pepperoni slices (about 35 slices), quartered

½ cup pizza sauce, plus additional for dipping

1 egg, beaten

||||||||||||||||||||||||||||||||||||||||||||||||||||||||||||||||||||||

1. Preheat oven to 350°F. Line baking sheet with parchment paper.

2. Separate biscuits; set aside one biscuit for decorations. Roll out remaining biscuits into 7-inch circles on lightly floured surface.

3. Top half of each circle evenly with cheese, mushrooms, pepperoni and ½ cup sauce, leaving ½-inch border. Fold dough over filling to form semicircle; seal edges with fork. Brush tops with egg.

4. Split remaining biscuit horizontally and cut each half into eight ¼-inch strips. For each sandwich, roll two strips of dough into spirals to create eyes. Divide remaining two strips of dough into seven pieces to create noses. Arrange eyes and noses on tops of sandwiches; brush with egg. Place on prepared baking sheet.

5. Bake 20 to 25 minutes or until golden brown. Cool on wire rack 5 minutes. Serve with additional pizza sauce.

TIP: Don't worry about leaking sauce or cheese—it will look like it's coming from the monster's mouth!

Skillet "Spaghetti" Toss

Makes 3 to 4 servings

2 tablespoons olive oil

1 cup sliced mushrooms

1 cup broccoli florets

2 Italian chicken sausages, sliced

2 packages (3 ounces each) ramen noodles, any flavor,* broken in half

1 to 1½ cups marinara pasta sauce

Grated Parmesan cheese

Discard seasoning packets.

1. Heat oil in large skillet over medium-high heat. Add mushrooms, broccoli and sausage; cook and stir 10 minutes or until broccoli is crisp-tender.

2. Meanwhile, cook noodles in medium saucepan of boiling water 2 minutes; drain well.

3. Add pasta sauce and noodles to skillet; toss to coat. Reduce heat to medium; cook until heated through. Top with cheese.

Snacks & Sides

Tickle Sticks

Makes 4 to 6 servings

1 pound watermelon	2 teaspoons honey
1 container (6 ounces) low-fat plain yogurt	Grated peel and juice of 1 lime

1. Cut watermelon into sticks about 3 inches long and ½ inch in diameter. Remove and discard seeds.

2. Combine yogurt, honey, lime peel and lime juice in small bowl. Serve with watermelon sticks.

Mac and Cheese
Mini Cups

Makes 36 cups

||||||||||||||||||||||||||||||||||||||||||||||||||||||||||||||||||||

- 3 tablespoons butter, divided
- 2 tablespoons all-purpose flour
- 1 cup milk
- 1 teaspoon salt
- ½ teaspoon black pepper
- 1 cup (4 ounces) shredded sharp Cheddar cheese
- 1 cup (4 ounces) shredded Muenster cheese
- 8 ounces elbow macaroni, cooked and drained
- ⅓ cup panko or plain dry bread crumbs
- Finely chopped fresh parsley (optional)

||||||||||||||||||||||||||||||||||||||||||||||||||||||||||||||||||||

1. Preheat oven to 400°F. Melt 1 tablespoon butter in large saucepan over medium heat; grease 36 mini (1¾-inch) muffin cups with melted butter.

2. Melt remaining 2 tablespoons butter in same saucepan over medium heat. Whisk in flour; cook and stir 2 minutes. Add milk, salt and pepper; cook and stir 3 minutes or until thickened. Remove from heat; stir in cheeses. Fold in macaroni. Divide mixture among prepared muffin cups; sprinkle with panko.

3. Bake about 25 minutes or until golden brown. Cool in pans 10 minutes; remove carefully using sharp knife. Garnish with parsley.

Crunchy Parmesan Zucchini Sticks

Makes 6 servings

||||||||||||||||||||||||||||||||||||||||||||||||||||||||||||||||||||||||

- 3 medium zucchini
- 1 package (3 ounces) ramen noodles, any flavor*
- ½ cup shredded Parmesan cheese
- ½ cup all-purpose flour
- 1 egg
- 1 tablespoon water

  Prepared marinara sauce for dipping

*Or substitute 1 cup regular or panko bread crumbs mixed with ½ teaspoon dried Italian seasoning.

||||||||||||||||||||||||||||||||||||||||||||||||||||||||||||||||||||||||

1. Preheat oven to 400°F. Line baking sheet with parchment paper. Cut zucchini in half crosswise, then cut each half into 4 sticks.

2. Place noodles and cheese in food processor; pulse until fine crumbs form. Pour into shallow dish.

3. Place flour and seasoning packet from noodles in another shallow dish; stir to combine. Whisk egg and water in third shallow dish. Line dishes up for dipping.

4. Coat zucchini sticks with flour. Dip in egg, letting excess drip back into dish. Roll in noodle mixture to coat. Place on prepared baking sheet. Repeat with remaining zucchini and ingredients.

5. Bake 20 minutes or until zucchini is softened and coating is golden brown. Serve warm with marinara sauce for dipping.

Butternut Squash Oven Chips

Makes 4 servings

||||||||||||||||||||||||||||||||||||||||||||||||||||||||||||||||||||||||||

Lime Yogurt Dip (recipe follows)

½ teaspoon garlic powder

¼ teaspoon salt

¼ teaspoon ground red pepper

1 butternut squash (about 2½ pounds), peeled, seeded and cut crosswise into 3-inch thin slices

2 teaspoons vegetable oil

||||||||||||||||||||||||||||||||||||||||||||||||||||||||||||||||||||||||||

1. Preheat oven to 425°F. Prepare Lime Yogurt Dip. Combine garlic powder, salt and ground red pepper in small bowl.

2. Using spiralizer, spiral butternut squash with thick spiral blade and cut in half. Or cut squash in half lengthwise and thinly slice with mandoline or sharp knife. Spread squash on baking sheet. Drizzle with oil and sprinkle with seasoning mix; gently toss to coat. Arrange in single layer.

3. Bake 20 to 25 minutes or until squash is browned and crisp, turning occasionally.

LIME YOGURT DIP: Combine ¼ cup reduced-fat mayonnaise, ¼ cup reduced-fat Greek yogurt, 1 teaspoon lime juice and ¼ teaspoon grated lime peel in small bowl. Refrigerate until ready to serve.

Snake Snacks

Makes 2 servings

|||||||||||||||||||||||||||||||||||||||||||||||||||||||||||||||||||

2 small ripe bananas

1 tablespoon fresh
   lemon juice

10 to 12 medium fresh
    strawberries, hulled

2 small fresh
   strawberries, hulled

|||||||||||||||||||||||||||||||||||||||||||||||||||||||||||||||||||

1. Peel and cut bananas crosswise into ¼-inch slices. Place in medium bowl; toss gently with lemon juice to prevent bananas from turning brown.

2. Leave 2 medium strawberries whole; cut remaining medium strawberries crosswise into ¼-inch slices.

3. Place whole strawberries on serving plates for heads; alternate banana and strawberry slices behind heads to form snakes. Arrange small strawberries at ends of snakes.

4. Cut 4 small pieces of banana for eyes; arrange on snake heads. Cut extra strawberry pieces into tongues if desired.

> **TIP:** Try to choose strawberries that are about the same diameter as the banana so all the fruit slices that make up the snake will be close to the same width.

Soft Pretzel Bites with Creamy Honey Mustard

Makes 12 servings

||||||||||||||||||||||||||||||||||||||||||||||||||||||||||||||||||||||||||

- ¾ cup reduced-fat sour cream
- ¼ cup Dijon mustard
- 3 tablespoons honey
- 1⅔ cups warm water (110° to 115°F)
- 1 package (¼ ounce) active dry yeast
- 2 teaspoons sugar
- 1 teaspoon table salt
- 4½ cups all-purpose flour, plus additional for work surface
- 2 tablespoons butter, softened
- Vegetable oil
- 12 cups water
- ½ cup baking soda
- Kosher salt

||||||||||||||||||||||||||||||||||||||||||||||||||||||||||||||||||||||||||

1. For creamy honey mustard, stir sour cream, mustard and honey in small bowl until smooth and well blended. Cover and refrigerate until ready to use.

2. Whisk 1⅔ cups warm water, yeast, sugar and table salt in large bowl. Let stand 5 minutes or until bubbly.

3. Add 4½ cups flour and butter to yeast mixture; beat with electric mixer at low speed until combined, scraping sides of bowl occasionally. Replace paddle attachment with dough hook. Beat at medium speed 5 minutes. Shape dough into a ball. Place in large lightly greased bowl; turn to grease top. Cover and let rise in warm place 1 hour or until doubled.

4. Preheat oven to 450°F. Generously brush baking sheets with vegetable oil. Bring 12 cups water to a boil in large saucepan.

5. Punch down dough; transfer to floured work surface. Flatten and stretch dough into 12 equal pieces. Roll each piece into 12-inch-long rope. Cut each rope into eight equal pieces.

6. Stir baking soda into boiling water until dissolved. Working in batches, drop dough into boiling water; boil 30 seconds. Transfer to prepared baking sheets using slotted spoon.

7. Sprinkle pieces evenly with kosher salt. Bake 12 minutes or until golden brown, rotating baking sheets halfway through baking. Serve with creamy honey mustard.

Crispy Green Bean Fries

Makes 6 servings

|||||||||||||||||||||||||||||||||||||||||||||||||||||||||||||||||||||

1 egg

1 pound green beans, ends trimmed

½ cup dry bread crumbs

¼ cup grated Parmesan cheese

1 tablespoon olive oil

½ teaspoon garlic powder

¼ teaspoon salt

Prepared ranch dressing (optional)

|||||||||||||||||||||||||||||||||||||||||||||||||||||||||||||||||||||

1. Preheat oven to 425°F. Line large baking sheet with parchment paper.

2. Whisk egg in large bowl. Add green beans; toss to coat. Combine bread crumbs, cheese, oil, garlic powder and salt in small bowl. Sprinkle bread crumb mixture over green beans. Spread green beans on prepared baking sheet in single layer.

3. Bake 12 minutes. Toss. Bake 10 minutes or until crispy. Serve with dressing, if desired.

Whole Grain Quackers

Makes about 12 crackers

½ cup plus 2 tablespoons old-fashioned oats	¼ cup milk
½ cup whole wheat flour	2 tablespoons honey
½ teaspoon salt	Sea salt or cinnamon sugar (optional)
¼ cup (½ stick) cold butter, cut into pieces	

1. Preheat oven to 375°F. Line baking sheet with parchment paper. Place oats in bowl of food processor; pulse until coarse flour forms.

2. Add whole wheat flour and salt; pulse to combine. Add butter; pulse until pea-size pieces form. Heat milk with honey in small microwavable measuring cup on HIGH 45 seconds or until honey dissolves.

3. Add milk mixture through feed tube of processor with motor running; process about 1 minute or until dough forms on top of blade. Transfer to lightly floured surface.

4. Roll dough with floured rolling pin very thin (1/16 inch). Cut small duck or other shapes with cookie cutters; transfer to baking sheet. Sprinkle with sea salt or cinnamon sugar, if desired.

5. Bake 6 to 8 minutes or until crackers are lightly browned. Cool on wire rack.

Sweet Potato Fries

Makes 2 servings

||||||||||||||||||||||||||||||||||||||||||||||||||||||||||||||||||||

1 large sweet potato
    (about 8 ounces)

2 teaspoons olive oil

¼ teaspoon coarse salt

¼ teaspoon black pepper

¼ teaspoon ground red
    pepper

Honey or maple syrup
    (optional)

||||||||||||||||||||||||||||||||||||||||||||||||||||||||||||||||||||

1. Preheat oven to 425°F. Spray baking sheet with nonstick cooking spray.

2. Peel sweet potato; cut lengthwise into long spears. Toss with oil, salt, black pepper and ground red pepper on prepared baking sheet. Arrange sweet potato spears in single layer not touching.

3. Bake 20 to 30 minutes or until lightly browned, turning halfway through baking time. Serve with honey, if desired.

Cinnamon Toast Poppers

Makes 12 servings

6 cups fresh bread* cubes (1-inch cubes)

2 tablespoons butter, melted

1 tablespoon plus 1½ teaspoons sugar

½ teaspoon ground cinnamon

Use a firm sourdough, whole wheat or semolina bread.

1. Preheat oven to 325°F. Place bread cubes in large bowl. Drizzle with butter; toss to coat.

2. Combine sugar and cinnamon in small bowl. Sprinkle over bread cubes; mix well. Spread bread cubes in single layer on ungreased baking sheet.

3. Bake 25 minutes or until bread is golden and fragrant, stirring once or twice. Serve warm or at room temperature.

Crispy Oven Fries with Herbed Dipping Sauce

Makes 3 servings

Herbed Dipping Sauce (recipe follows)	2 tablespoons vegetable oil
2 large baking potatoes	1 teaspoon kosher salt

1. Preheat oven to 425°F. Spray two baking sheets with nonstick cooking spray. Prepare Herbed Dipping Sauce.

2. Cut potatoes lengthwise into ¼-inch slices, then cut each slice into ¼-inch strips. Combine potato strips and oil on prepared baking sheets. Toss to coat evenly; arrange in single layer.

3. Bake 25 minutes. Turn fries over; bake 15 minutes or until light golden brown and crisp. Sprinkle with salt. Serve immediately with Herbed Dipping Sauce.

HERBED DIPPING SAUCE: Stir ½ cup mayonnaise, 2 tablespoons chopped fresh herbs (such as basil, parsley, oregano and/or dill), 1 teaspoon salt and ½ teaspoon black pepper in small bowl until smooth and well blended. Cover and refrigerate until ready to serve.

Smoothies

Blueberry and Banana Frozen Yogurt Smoothie

Makes 2 servings

||||||||||||||||||||||||||||||||||||||||||||||||||||||||||||||||||

1½ cups fresh or frozen blueberries

1 banana

1 cup milk

1 cup vanilla frozen yogurt

||||||||||||||||||||||||||||||||||||||||||||||||||||||||||||||||||

1. Combine blueberries, banana and milk in blender; blend until smooth.

2. Add frozen yogurt; blend until smooth. Pour into two glasses. Serve immediately.

Creamy Fruit Blend

Makes 2 servings

|||||||||||||||||||||||||||||||||||||||||||||||||||||||||||||||||||||||

1 medium banana, peeled and quartered

1 cup milk

1 small ripe peach, peeled, pitted and quartered

½ cup fresh or frozen unsweetened strawberries

½ cup white grape juice

2 tablespoons packed brown sugar

1 tablespoon lemon juice

½ teaspoon almond extract

|||||||||||||||||||||||||||||||||||||||||||||||||||||||||||||||||||||||

1. Combine banana, milk, peach, strawberries, grape juice, brown sugar, lemon juice and almond extract in blender. Blend until smooth.

2. Pour into two glasses. Serve immediately.

Peaches and Green

Makes 2 servings

IIIIIIIIIIIIIIIIIIIIIIIIIIIIIIIIIIIIIIIIIIIIIIIIIIIIIIIIIIIIIIIIIIIIIII

¾ cup almond milk

1 cup packed fresh spinach

1 cup frozen peach slices

1 cup ice cubes

1 tablespoon honey

⅛ teaspoon vanilla

IIIIIIIIIIIIIIIIIIIIIIIIIIIIIIIIIIIIIIIIIIIIIIIIIIIIIIIIIIIIIIIIIIIIIII

Combine almond milk, spinach, peaches, ice, honey and vanilla in blender; blend until smooth. Pour into two glasses. Serve immediately.

Tofu Orange Dream

Makes 1 serving

||||||||||||||||||||||||||||||||||||||||||||||||||||||||||||||||||||||||||

½ cup (4 ounces) soft tofu

½ cup orange juice

1 container (about 2½ ounces) baby food carrots

2 tablespoons honey *or* 1 tablespoon sugar

¼ teaspoon grated fresh ginger

2 to 3 ice cubes

||||||||||||||||||||||||||||||||||||||||||||||||||||||||||||||||||||||||||

1. Combine tofu, orange juice, carrots, honey, ginger and ice in blender. Blend 15 seconds or until smooth.

2. Pour into glass. Serve immediately.

Raspberry Smoothie

Makes 2 servings

||||||||||||||||||||||||||||||||||||||||||||||||||||||||||||||||||||||||||||

1½ **cups fresh or frozen raspberries, plus additional for garnish**

1 **cup plain nonfat yogurt**

4 **teaspoons sugar**

1 **tablespoon honey**

1 **cup crushed ice**

||||||||||||||||||||||||||||||||||||||||||||||||||||||||||||||||||||||||||||

1. Combine 1½ cups raspberries, yogurt, sugar, honey and ice in blender; blend until smooth.

2. Pour into two glasses. Serve immediately.

Sunny Mango Sipper

Makes 3 servings

||||||||||||||||||||||||||||||||||||||||||||||||||||||||||||||||||||

1 cup frozen mango chunks

1 container (6 ounces) vanilla low-fat yogurt

½ cup orange juice

1 tablespoon honey

||||||||||||||||||||||||||||||||||||||||||||||||||||||||||||||||||||

1. Combine mango chunks, yogurt, orange juice and honey in blender. Cover; blend until smooth, pulsing to break up mango chunks.

2. Pour into three glasses. Serve immediately.

Rainbow Party Smoothies

Makes 3 servings

|||||||||||||||||||||||||||||||||||||||||||||||||||||||||||||||||||

1½ cups fruit punch

⅓ cup rainbow sherbet

½ cup club soda

Additional rainbow sherbet (optional)

|||||||||||||||||||||||||||||||||||||||||||||||||||||||||||||||||||

1. Combine fruit punch and ⅓ cup sherbet in blender. Process until smooth. Pour into three glasses; add club soda.

2. Top with additional sherbet, if desired.

Peanut Butter Banana Blend

Makes 2 servings

|||||||||||||||||||||||||||||||||||||||||||||||||||||||||||||||||||||||||||||||||

1 frozen banana

½ cup plain yogurt

½ cup milk

1 tablespoon natural unsweetened peanut butter

|||||||||||||||||||||||||||||||||||||||||||||||||||||||||||||||||||||||||||||||||

1. Combine banana, yogurt, milk and peanut butter in blender; blend until smooth.

2. Pour into two glasses. Serve immediately.

Rise and Shine Smoothie

Makes 2 servings

IIIIIIIIIIIIIIIIIIIIIIIIIIIIIIIIIIIIIIIIIIIIIIIIIIIIIIIIII

½ cup uncooked old-fashioned oats

1 cup orange juice

1 container (6 ounces) vanilla yogurt

½ cup vanilla soy milk

4 whole strawberries

3 ice cubes

½ teaspoon ground cinnamon (optional)

IIIIIIIIIIIIIIIIIIIIIIIIIIIIIIIIIIIIIIIIIIIIIIIIIIIIIIIIII

1. Pour oats into blender; grind into fine crumbs.

2. Add orange juice, yogurt, soy milk, strawberries, ice and cinnamon, if desired, to blender. Process until thoroughly blended.

3. Pour into two glasses. Serve immediately.

Tropical Breakfast Smoothie

Makes 4 servings

1 can (20 ounces) pineapple chunks in juice, undrained

1 ripe banana

½ cup ice cubes

½ cup orange juice

¼ cup flaked coconut

1 tablespoon fresh lime juice

Maraschino cherries and lime wedges (optional)

1. Combine pineapple, banana, ice, orange juice, coconut and lime juice in blender; blend until smooth.

2. Pour into four glasses. Garnish with cherries and lime wedges. Serve immediately.

Berry-Banana Breakfast Smoothie

Makes 2 servings

||||||||||||||||||||||||||||||||||||||||||||||||||||||||||||||||||

1 container (6 ounces) berry-flavored low-fat yogurt

1 ripe banana, sliced

½ cup milk

||||||||||||||||||||||||||||||||||||||||||||||||||||||||||||||||||

Place yogurt, banana and milk in blender; blend until smooth. Pour into two glasses. Serve immediately.

Creamy Strawberry–Banana Shake

Makes 2 servings

1½ cups ice cubes	½ cup orange juice
½ banana	¼ avocado
½ cup fresh strawberries, hulled	

1. Combine ice, banana, strawberries, orange juice and avocado in blender; blend until smooth.

2. Pour into two glasses. Serve immediately.

Treats

Choco-Peanut Butter Popcorn

Makes 6 servings

||||||||||||||||||||||||||||||||||||||||||||||||||||||||||||||||||||||||

⅓ cup semisweet
chocolate chips

3 tablespoons natural
creamy peanut
butter

1 tablespoon butter

4 cups air-popped
popcorn

½ cup powdered sugar

||||||||||||||||||||||||||||||||||||||||||||||||||||||||||||||||||||||||

1. Microwave chocolate chips, peanut butter and butter in medium microwavable bowl on HIGH 30 seconds; stir. Microwave 30 seconds or until melted and smooth. Pour mixture over popcorn in large bowl, stirring until evenly coated. Transfer to 1-gallon resealable food storage bag.

2. Add powdered sugar to bag; seal bag and shake until well coated. Spread onto waxed paper to cool. Store leftovers in airtight container in refrigerator.

Dreamy Orange Creamy Pops

Makes 8 pops

|||||||||||||||||||||||||||||||||||||||||||||||||||||||||||||||||||||

2 cups ice

1½ cups vanilla yogurt

¾ cup frozen orange juice concentrate

½ cup milk

¼ teaspoon vanilla

Pop molds with lids

|||||||||||||||||||||||||||||||||||||||||||||||||||||||||||||||||||||

1. Combine ice, yogurt, orange juice concentrate, milk and vanilla in blender or food processor; blend until smooth.

2. Pour mixture into molds. Cover with lids. Freeze 6 hours or until firm.

3. To remove pops from molds, place bottoms of pops under warm running water until loosened. Press firmly on bottoms to release. (Do not twist or pull lids.)

TIP: Frozen juice concentrate works great for frozen pops. Try any desired juice flavor and pair it with yogurt for a creamy fruity treat.

My Own Berry Pie

Makes 3 servings

||||||||||||||||||||||||||||||||||||||||||||||||||||||||||||||||

1 refrigerated pie crust (half of 15-ounce package)

2 cups fresh or frozen blueberries

2 tablespoons sugar, plus additional for topping

2 tablespoons all-purpose flour

1 teaspoon lemon peel

¼ teaspoon vanilla

¼ teaspoon ground cinnamon

1 tablespoon butter, cut into small pieces

1 egg

1 teaspoon water

||||||||||||||||||||||||||||||||||||||||||||||||||||||||||||||||

1. Preheat oven to 375°F. Spray three ovenproof jars, mugs or ramekins with nonstick cooking spray.

2. Cut pie crust into six equal pieces. Press one piece into bottom of each prepared jar.

3. Combine blueberries, 2 tablespoons sugar, flour, lemon peel, vanilla and cinnamon in medium bowl; toss gently to coat. Spoon mixture over crusts in jars; dot with butter.

4. Cut remaining three pieces of dough into ½-inch strips. Arrange strips in lattice design over top of each jar; press ends of strips securely to seal. Beat egg and water in small bowl; brush over lattice. Sprinkle with additional sugar. Place jars on baking sheet.

5. Bake 40 to 45 minutes or until crusts are golden brown. Let stand 10 to 15 minutes before serving.

Frozen Chocolate Banana Pops

Makes 6 servings

| | | | | | | | | | | | | | | | | | | | | | | | | | | | | | | | | | | | | | | | | | | | | | | | | | | | | | | | | | | | | | | | | | | | | | | | | | | | | |

3 bananas, peeled

6 ice cream sticks or wooden skewers

½ cup semisweet chocolate chips

1½ teaspoons vegetable oil

¼ cup sprinkles, chopped peanuts, coconut or crushed cookies (optional)

| | | | | | | | | | | | | | | | | | | | | | | | | | | | | | | | | | | | | | | | | | | | | | | | | | | | | | | | | | | | | | | | | | | | | | | | | | | | | |

1. Line baking sheet with waxed paper or foil. Cut each banana in half. Insert wooden pop stick halfway into each banana. Place on prepared baking sheet; freeze 1 hour.

2. Combine chocolate chips and oil in small saucepan; stir over low heat until melted and smooth.

3. Remove bananas from freezer. Spoon chocolate over each banana while holding over saucepan. Sprinkle with desired toppings. Return to baking sheet; freeze about 1 hour or until chocolate and toppings are set. Store in airtight container or resealable freezer food storage bag.

NOTE: If desired, bananas can be cut into 1-inch pieces, frozen, then dipped in chocolate for individual bites.

Cinnamon Caramel Corn

Makes 4 servings

||||||||||||||||||||||||||||||||||||||||||||||||||||||||||||||||||||

- 8 cups air-popped popcorn (about ⅓ cup kernels)
- 2 tablespoons honey
- 4 teaspoons butter
- ¼ teaspoon ground cinnamon

||||||||||||||||||||||||||||||||||||||||||||||||||||||||||||||||||||

1. Preheat oven to 350°F. Spray jelly-roll pan with nonstick cooking spray. Place popcorn in large bowl.

2. Combine honey, butter and cinnamon in small saucepan; cook and stir over low heat until butter is melted and mixture is smooth. Immediately pour over popcorn; toss to coat evenly. Pour onto prepared pan.

3. Bake 12 to 14 minutes or until coating is golden brown and appears crackled, stirring twice.

4. Cool popcorn on pan. (As popcorn cools, coating becomes crisp. If not crisp enough, or if popcorn softens upon standing, return to oven and heat 5 to 8 minutes.) Store in airtight container.

CAJUN POPCORN: Preheat oven and prepare jelly-roll pan as directed above. Replace cinnamon with 1 teaspoon Cajun or Creole seasoning and add 1 extra teaspoon honey. Proceed with recipe as directed above.

ITALIAN POPCORN: Spray 8 cups air-popped popcorn with butter-flavored cooking spray to coat. Sprinkle with 2 tablespoons grated Parmesan cheese, ½ teaspoon dried oregano and ⅛ teaspoon black pepper. Gently toss to coat. Bake as directed.

Fruit Salad with Creamy Banana Dressing

Makes 8 servings

||||||||||||||||||||||||||||||||||||||||||||||||||||||||||||||||

- 2 cups fresh pineapple chunks
- 1 cup cantaloupe cubes
- 1 cup honeydew melon cubes
- 1 cup fresh blackberries
- 1 cup sliced fresh strawberries
- 1 cup seedless red grapes
- 1 medium apple, diced
- 2 medium ripe bananas, sliced
- ½ cup nonfat Greek yogurt
- 2 tablespoons honey
- 1 tablespoon lemon juice
- ¼ teaspoon ground nutmeg

||||||||||||||||||||||||||||||||||||||||||||||||||||||||||||||||

1. Combine pineapple, cantaloupe, honeydew, blackberries, strawberries, grapes and apple in large bowl; gently mix.

2. Combine bananas, yogurt, honey, lemon juice and nutmeg in blender or food processor; blend until smooth.

3. Pour dressing over fruit mixture; gently toss to coat evenly. Serve immediately.

Cranberry Chocolate Chip Cereal Squares

Makes about 30 squares

||||||||||||||||||||||||||||||||||||||||||||||||||||||||||||||||||||||||||||||||

6½ cups corn or rice cereal squares, divided

1 package (6 ounces) dried cranberries (about 1⅓ cups)

½ cup (1 stick) butter

1 package (about 10 ounces) mini marshmallows

1 cup semisweet chocolate chips

||||||||||||||||||||||||||||||||||||||||||||||||||||||||||||||||||||||||||||||||

1. Line 13×9-inch baking pan with foil, leaving 2-inch overhang on two sides. Spray with nonstick cooking spray.

2. Coarsely crush 2 cups cereal in large bowl with back of spoon or hands. Stir in cranberries.

3. Melt butter in large saucepan over low heat. Add marshmallows; stir constantly until marshmallows are melted and mixture is smooth. Remove from heat; stir in remaining 4½ cups whole cereal and crushed cereal mixture until well blended. Stir in chocolate chips. Press mixture into prepared pan.

4. Cover and refrigerate 30 minutes or until firm. Remove from pan using foil; cut into squares.

Paradise Pops

Makes 4 pops

||||||||||||||||||||||||||||||||||||||||||||||||||||||||||||||||||||||||||

1 cup milk

¾ cup frozen or fresh pineapple chunks

¾ cup frozen or fresh mango chunks

¼ cup unsweetened coconut milk

1 tablespoon honey

Pop molds or paper or plastic cups

Pop sticks

||||||||||||||||||||||||||||||||||||||||||||||||||||||||||||||||||||||||||

1. Combine milk, pineapple, mango, coconut milk and honey in blender or food processor; blend until smooth.

2. Pour mixture into molds. Cover top of each mold with small piece of foil. Freeze 1 hour.

3. Insert sticks through center of foil. Freeze 6 hours or until firm.

4. To remove pops from molds, remove foil and place bottoms of pops under warm running water until loosened. Press firmly on bottoms to release. (Do not twist or pull sticks.)

Chocolate-Drizzled Grape Skewers

Makes 6 servings

||||||||||||||||||||||||||||||||||||||||||||||||||||||||||||||||||||||||||

2 cups seedless grapes
   (green, red or a
   combination of both)

Bamboo skewers

¼ cup semisweet
   chocolate chips

¼ cup white chocolate
   chips

||||||||||||||||||||||||||||||||||||||||||||||||||||||||||||||||||||||||||

1. Wash grapes; remove stems. Dry completely with paper towel. Thread grapes onto skewers. Place on waxed paper-lined baking sheet (see Tip).

2. Place semisweet chocolate chips in small microwavable bowl; microwave on HIGH 1 minute. Stir. Microwave at 30-second intervals, stirring after each interval until smooth. Drizzle over grapes.

3. Place white chocolate chips in separate small microwavable bowl; microwave on HIGH 1 minute. Stir. Microwave at 30-second intervals, stirring after each interval until smooth. Drizzle over grapes.

4. Freeze at least 2 hours before serving.

TIP: Use a rimmed baking sheet for this recipe. Rest the bamboo skewers against the rims and rotate them on the baking sheet to drizzle evenly with chocolate.

VARIATION: You can also freeze the grapes completely and drizzle them with chocolate just before serving.

Cherry-Peach Pops

Makes 7 servings

⅓ cup peach or apricot nectar

1 teaspoon unflavored gelatin

1 can (15 ounces) sliced peaches in light syrup, drained

1 carton (6 ounces) peach or cherry yogurt

1 carton (6 ounces) cherry yogurt

7 (3-ounce) paper cups

Wooden pop sticks

1. Combine nectar and gelatin in small saucepan; let stand 5 minutes. Cook and stir over low heat just until gelatin dissolves.

2. Combine nectar mixture, peaches and yogurts in blender or food processor; blend until smooth.

3. Pour into cups, filling each about two-thirds full. Place in freezer; freeze 1 hour. Insert pop stick into center of each cup. Freeze at least 3 more hours.

4. Let stand at room temperature 10 minutes before serving. Tear away paper cups to serve.

Mini Tartes Tatin

Makes 6 servings

||||||||||||||||||||||||||||||||||||||||||||||||||||||||||||||||||||||||||||||||||

5 small sweet-tart apples such as Pink Lady or Honeycrisp,* peeled, cored and slice crosswise into ⅛-inch-thick rounds

2 tablespoons granulated sugar

1 teaspoon ground cinnamon

3 tablespoons butter

2 tablespoons packed brown sugar

1 refrigerated pie crust (half of 15-ounce package)

Whipped cream (optional)

Look for apples that are about the size of standard muffin pan cups, about 2 to 2½ inches in diameter and 5 to 6 ounces each.

||||||||||||||||||||||||||||||||||||||||||||||||||||||||||||||||||||||||||||||||||

1. Preheat oven to 350°F. Spray 6 standard (2½-inch) nonstick muffin cups with nonstick cooking spray.

2. Combine apple slices, granulated sugar and cinnamon in large bowl; toss to coat.

3. Place ½ tablespoon butter in each prepared muffin cup. Top with 1 teaspoon brown sugar, spreading to cover bottom of cup. Stack apple rings in cups, packing down to fit; fill center holes with broken or small apple slices. (Stacks will be tall and extend about 1 inch above rim of cup.) Place pan on rimmed baking sheet; cover loosely with foil.

4. Bake 25 minutes (apples will sink slightly and be crisp-tender).

5. Meanwhile, let pie crust stand at room temperature 15 minutes. Unroll crust on work surface; cut out 6 circles with 2½- to 3-inch biscuit cutter.

6. Place one dough circle on top of each stack of apples, pressing slightly around apples. Bake, uncovered, 20 minutes or until crust is light golden brown. Cool in pan 3 minutes. Place cutting board on top of pan and invert. Carefully remove muffin pan; transfer tarts to individual serving plate. Serve warm with whipped cream, if desired.

Metric Conversion Chart

||||||||||||||||||||||||||||||||||||||||||||||||||||||||||||||

VOLUME MEASUREMENTS (dry)

1/8 teaspoon = 0.5 mL
1/4 teaspoon = 1 mL
1/2 teaspoon = 2 mL
3/4 teaspoon = 4 mL
1 teaspoon = 5 mL
1 tablespoon = 15 mL
2 tablespoons = 30 mL
1/4 cup = 60 mL
1/3 cup = 75 mL
1/2 cup = 125 mL
2/3 cup = 150 mL
3/4 cup = 175 mL
1 cup = 250 mL
2 cups = 1 pint = 500 mL
3 cups = 750 mL
4 cups = 1 quart = 1 L

VOLUME MEASUREMENTS (fluid)

1 fluid ounce (2 tablespoons) = 30 mL
4 fluid ounces (1/2 cup) = 125 mL
8 fluid ounces (1 cup) = 250 mL
12 fluid ounces (1 1/2 cups) = 375 mL
16 fluid ounces (2 cups) = 500 mL

WEIGHTS (mass)

1/2 ounce = 15 g
1 ounce = 30 g
3 ounces = 90 g
4 ounces = 120 g
8 ounces = 225 g
10 ounces = 285 g
12 ounces = 360 g
16 ounces = 1 pound = 450 g

DIMENSIONS

1/16 inch = 2 mm
1/8 inch = 3 mm
1/4 inch = 6 mm
1/2 inch = 1.5 cm
3/4 inch = 2 cm
1 inch = 2.5 cm

OVEN TEMPERATURES

250°F = 120°C
275°F = 140°C
300°F = 150°C
325°F = 160°C
350°F = 180°C
375°F = 190°C
400°F = 200°C
425°F = 220°C
450°F = 230°C

BAKING PAN SIZES

Utensil	Size in Inches/Quarts	Metric Volume	Size in Centimeters
Baking or	8×8×2	2 L	20×20×5
Cake Pan	9×9×2	2.5 L	23×23×5
(square or	12×8×2	3 L	30×20×5
rectangular)	13×9×2	3.5 L	33×23×5
Loaf Pan	8×4×3	1.5 L	20×10×7
	9×5×3	2 L	23×13×7
Round Layer	8×1½	1.2 L	20×4
Cake Pan	9×1½	1.5 L	23×4
Pie Plate	8×1¼	750 mL	20×3
	9×1¼	1 L	23×3
Baking Dish	1 quart	1 L	—
or Casserole	1½ quart	1.5 L	—
	2 quart	2 L	—